THE 5-MINUTE MOTIVATIONAL JOURNAL

THE 5-MINUTE MOTIVATIONAL JOURNAL

Daily Prompts to Achieve Your Goals and Live Intentionally

DR. CHRISTIAN RIZEA, PSYD

ROCKRIDGE
PRESS

For general information on our other products and services or to obtain technical support, please contact our Customer Care Department within the United States at (866) 744-2665, or outside the United States at (510) 253-0500.

Rockridge Press publishes its books in a variety of electronic and print formats. Some content that appears in print may not be available in electronic books, and vice versa.

Interior and Cover Designer: Stephanie Sumulong
Art Producer: Janice Ackerman
Editor: Jesse Aylen
Production Editor: Andrew Yackira
Production Manager: Giraud Lorber
Author photo: Christina Hernandez

ISBN: Print 978-1-64876-835-4

R0

For my parents and brother, Corneliu, Maria, and Bogdan Rizea, as well as my wife, Sasha. Thank you!

CONTENTS

INTRODUCTION

I'm thrilled that you're here and have decided to take the plunge into greater self-discovery and personal growth to achieve your dreams. You likely picked up this journal because you feel your pent-up desires, goals, and greater purpose are waiting to be unleashed, or perhaps you've plateaued, lost passion, or are unsure how to get to the next level in your career, relationships, creativity, or health goals. If any of these ring true, then this is the journal for you.

The 5-Minute Motivational Journal is specifically designed to empower you to literally be the author of your own destiny by helping you increase your confidence, set goals, engage your talents and passions, and interact with your community, all in an organically authentic and motivated way.

My name is Dr. Christian Rizea, and I'm a psychologist with the life purpose to provide people the tools to live with self-determination, a greater sense of personal fulfillment, and the ability to achieve their dreams. I've had the privilege of helping a wide range of populations, from incarcerated individuals to people living with chronic illnesses, to individuals who've survived traumatic life experiences. I take a holistic approach to healing and self-actualization by using hypnotherapy, cognitive behavioral therapy, and spiritual conceptualizations to treat individuals.

When I was 31 years old, I was living in a studio apartment, and my life wasn't going as planned. I had aspirations that weren't materializing, and I wanted to leave my mark by having a greater impact on people's lives. I felt like I was trying to move forward but the brakes were on, which left me feeling frustrated. Then one night, rummaging through a box of old books, I serendipitously found *Awaken the Giant Within* by Tony Robbins. Boy, did it light a fire within me! I became obsessed with motivation as the mechanism that would help me and the people I work with in my practice get what we want out of life.

But what is motivation? Simply put, motivation is an internal process that inspires you to take action on a clearly identified need or want. It was motivation that energized Kobe Bryant to wake up every day at five a.m. to make 2,000 shots, it was motivation that directed Marie Curie to become the first female professor at the University of Paris, and it was motivation that kept Michelangelo painting the Sistine Chapel for four years. When you harness the magic of motivation, your energy, direction, and persistence will flow through you to help you lead a more fulfilling life.

In this journal, I've created prompts and exercises that use the top psychological research on motivation and proven techniques from peak performance leaders to guide you through five-minute journal entries. Through the tested power of motivation, this journal will enable your personal growth, making it achievable and accessible. You'll find that each section includes prompts, exercises, and affirmations engineered to gradually dissolve your limiting barriers and build the skills and qualities you need to create the life you want. You'll be challenged to become more self-aware, internalize constructive habits, and execute powerful life hacks that are aligned with your authentic self—all in just five minutes a day.

Are you ready to unlock your true potential and seize your dreams? Of course you are! By the end of this journal, you'll have greater insight into your true self. You'll have strategies for how to make your unique vision come into reality and will take action on manifesting them into the world. I'm excited to be with you on this journey of self-discovery and achievement, so let's get going!

PART ONE

FIND YOUR MOTIVATION FROM WITHIN

You possess all the psychological resources within you to support personal growth and achieve your dreams. It's a matter of reflecting on your inner world and nurturing the resources you discover to get you where you want to be.

The foundation of your psychological resources is the relationship you have with yourself. This sacred relationship is expressed by your behavior in self-fulfilling prophecies. Self-esteem, self-confidence, and self-empowerment are psychological resources that reflect how you relate to yourself. If you have an unhealthy relationship with yourself, you won't feel deserving of your dreams and will be unmotivated to go after them, but a positive relationship with yourself will make your life feel limitless.

The relationship with yourself is shaped by so many factors, including your parental or familial upbringing and societal conditioning. I understand that you may have had adverse experiences growing up, but—hear me out— your past is not a life sentence! The beauty of your relationship with yourself is that it has unlimited possibilities for positive change and growth.

In this chapter, you will engage with prompts, exercises, quotations, and affirmations that attend to this relationship by helping you listen to your true inner voice, identify and cultivate your personal psychological resources, and learn about goals and how to build them. All of this will lay the groundwork for the activities in part 2.

"Without dreams and goals, there is no living, only merely existing, and that is not why we are here."

—Mark Twain

Self-compassion is the ability to recognize emotional pain within yourself and to approach it with the intention to alleviate it. You can alleviate pain through kindness, understanding, meeting your needs, and self-soothing behaviors. What does it mean for you to be more self-compassionate? What can you achieve with that greater sense of self-compassion?

_____

_____

_____

_____

_____

_____

_____

_____

_____

_____

With a nonjudgmental and open mind, reflect on the areas in your life where you could be more self-compassionate and what you need to alleviate some of the pain.

The pain I choose to alleviate with self-compassion is . . .

_____

_____

_____

I choose to be more self-compassionate about this because . . .

_____

_____

_____

Doing this today will help me with . . .

_____

_____

_____

Today, I will take care of this pain through self-compassion by doing . . .

_____

_____

_____

Your personality is composed of many parts. There's a part that falls in love, an anxious part, and a spontaneous part. You have thousands of different parts within you, and together, they guide your decisions and actions. Considering this, think about your self-compassionate part. Describe how your self-compassionate part looks, feels, makes decisions, and can help empower you through challenging times.

_____

_____

_____

_____

_____

_____

_____

_____

_____

_____

The four qualities of self-compassion are wisdom (i.e., knowledge and experience), strength, warmth, and responsibility. Elaborate on how you will tap in to these qualities to get one of your needs met today.

Through wisdom, I will . . . _____

_____

_____

Through strength, I will . . . _____

_____

_____

Through warmth, I will . . . _____

_____

_____

Through responsibility, I will . . . _____

_____

_____

Close your eyes and picture yourself taking on the emotions, thoughts, body postures, and even facial expressions of the self-compassionate part of your personality. Then imagine yourself taking the steps to meet your need and how wonderful you will feel afterward. Go forward in your day carrying that same energy.

"Self-compassion—being supportive and kind to yourself, especially in the face of stress and failure—is associated with more motivation and better self-control."

—Kelly McGonigal

As a reactive response, anxiety can be a major block to motivation. Anxiety can be so uncomfortable that it causes you to avoid, rather than approach, what you want. What goal is anxiety currently preventing you from reaching? How is anxiety preventing you from taking action?

Imagine you're watching a biographical film with yourself as the main character. Envision a scene set in the present time where anxiety is preventing the main character from pursuing the goal you described in the previous prompt. Now imagine that your compassionate self is the director of the film, guiding the main character to achieve the goal. Using the following prompts, visualize how the director would help the main character achieve the goal. Let that inform how you, in turn, approach your anxieties.

The director would normalize and validate the main character's feelings by saying . . .

To soothe the main character's anxiety, the director would say . . .

The director would remind the main character of the importance of achieving this goal by saying . . .

The director would tell the main character the first actionable steps to achieve this goal would be to . . .

At some point, we all have a critical voice inside of our head that lowers our self-esteem. Listening too intently to this critical voice has the consequence of preventing you from achieving your goals. No person is born with a critical voice. It develops from the messages received from caregivers, authority figures, and media-driven influences. What's an example of a critical voice you overcame? Thinking about your current goals, what's an example of an empowering inner voice that keeps you motivated?

_____

_____

_____

_____

_____

_____

_____

_____

_____

_____

_____

_____

_____

What current events are activating the critical voice that impedes you from taking action or completing a goal?

_____

_____

What does the critical voice say when activated?

_____

_____

Who does this critical voice remind you of?

_____

_____

How much do you believe the critical voice's statement about you?

_____

_____

Talk back to the critical voice and write a balanced, more reasonable response to the criticism.

_____

_____

*No matter the circumstance,
my inner motivating voice
supports me.*

It might seem paradoxical, but your critical voice has positive intentions behind it. The positive intention is usually to protect you from something, such as experiencing failure, but you still get hurt in the end. By uncovering the positive intent behind a critical voice, you remove its power to reduce your self-esteem. What's a current critical voice that's related to one of your goals? Looking at it through the unexpected lens of positivity, what is that critical voice trying to protect you from experiencing?

_____

_____

_____

_____

_____

_____

_____

_____

_____

_____

Let's unmask the hidden purpose of a critical voice that's currently getting in the way of achieving one of your goals. From the following assortment of choices, circle the purpose of a critical voice that's affecting your self-esteem and motivation, and write in your own words as well, if you'd like:

TO LIVE BY MY PARENTS',
FAMILY'S, OR
CAREGIVER'S RULES

TO PREVENT ME
FROM BEING REJECTED

TO REDUCE
ANXIETY

TO MAINTAIN COMFORT

TO MAINTAIN
PREDICTABILITY

TO PREVENT
EMBARRASSMENT

TO PREVENT FAILURE

TO LIVE UP TO SOMEONE
ELSE'S EXPECTATIONS OF ME

_____

_____

Now bring it all together by filling in the blanks:

"You're saying to me (critical voice)_____

so that I (hidden purpose)_____"

Considering what you've learned after doing this exercise, what are some ways you might push back against that critical voice to regain your motivation and drive?

_____

_____

_____

When you can't seem to get moving because critical thoughts are keeping you down, it helps to tap in to an inner motivating voice. This voice rebuts the critic. The inner motivating voice's persona can be an inspirational teacher, celebrity, coach, fictional character, real-life person, mentor, or wise elder who will stick up for you against your critical thoughts. Who will be your inner motivating voice? Why is this persona motivating to you?

_____

_____

_____

_____

_____

_____

_____

_____

_____

_____

_____

_____

_____

> **"Don't let the noise of others' opinions drown out your own inner voice."**
>
> **—Steve Jobs**

Sometimes your inner motivating voice isn't enough to fully let go of critical thoughts. In these moments, thought defusion can be a valuable tool to help you gain distance from your thoughts and empower your motivation. Thought defusion means to detach from your thoughts. Understand that you are not your thoughts but are a person having thoughts, which are merely words, ideas, and images in your mind. What's a critical thought you've recently been experiencing that is difficult to let go of?

_____

_____

_____

_____

_____

_____

_____

_____

_____

_____

As you've explored, defusion is a technique that works wonders by using imagery to let go of critical thoughts. To begin, write one of your critical thoughts.

_____

_____

_____

_____

_____

_____

_____

_____

_____

_____

_____

My favorite and most empowering defusion imagery technique is called "leaves on a stream." Picture yourself sitting next to a stream. Whatever critical thought comes up, place it on a leaf and watch it flow down the stream until you no longer see it. Do this with the critical thought you identified here and continue placing your critical thoughts on leaves for two minutes. Reflect on how it feels to watch your critical thoughts drift away, leaving you more empowered and intentional.

Values are a compass to guide how you want to move through life. Values should be life-enhancing, meaning that they encourage you to meet your needs. When your behaviors are aligned with your values, you generally feel good about your actions. Some common value domains include relationships, education, health, family, spirituality, creativity, and career. What are the most important values to you right now? Which value gets you feeling the most excited and why?

_____

_____

_____

_____

_____

_____

_____

_____

_____

_____

_____

_____

We all have values, called introjected values, that didn't originate from our authentic self but came early on in our lives from caregivers or societal conditioning. At a young age, we unquestioningly took on those values. But in adulthood, some of those values may not serve your goals. What's an example of an introjected value you still hold on to that's preventing you from achieving your goals? What are some values you hold that will help you achieve your goals?

_____

_____

_____

_____

_____

_____

_____

_____

_____

_____

_____

_____

_____

A former client of mine was overcoming alcohol addiction, and his primary value was health. When he was offered alcohol in social situations, he posed this question to himself: "Would drinking this alcohol make me aligned or unaligned with my value of health?" His decision to decline the alcohol was easier because he was guided by his primary value. Think for a moment about something you're struggling with right now. Then write down what kind of decisions will align your actions with your values.

_____

_____

_____

_____

_____

_____

_____

_____

_____

_____

_____

"*I have learned that as long as I hold fast to my beliefs and values—and follow my own moral compass—then the only expectations I need to live up to are my own.*"

—Michelle Obama

Create a "values contract" with yourself. Every day of this week, commit to act in alignment with a value that's relevant to a goal you want to achieve. As a promise to yourself to follow through, sign the contract at the end.

This week, I'm committed to my value of . . .
So that I can . . .
By taking these actions:

1. _____

_____

_____

2. _____

_____

_____

3. _____

_____

_____

Signed _____

When following through with your values contract, uncomfortable feelings may arise because you're breaking old habits and doing the opposite of what feels familiar. What are some uncomfortable feelings you expect to come up? What will you say to yourself to stay on course? What will you do to take care of yourself to tolerate those feelings? If you get sidetracked from your values contract, what will you do to get back on track?

_____

_____

_____

_____

_____

_____

_____

_____

_____

_____

_____

_____

We sometimes stop ourselves from pursuing a goal because we care about how other people perceive us. Whose opinions about you might be affecting your decision to follow through on a goal? What do you think will be the worst thing to happen if they have that opinion of you? Whose opinion do you respect, and what advice would they give you about pursuing your goals when facing adversity?

_____

_____

_____

_____

_____

_____

_____

_____

_____

_____

_____

_____

One decision can change your life! Making the wrong decision can lead to regret, but making the right one will lead to achieving what's in your heart. Think about one of your goals. What would you regret if you didn't follow through with it? What are the possible options to act on this goal? What are the pros and cons of each option? For the best option, what can you act on today?

_____

_____

_____

_____

_____

_____

_____

_____

_____

_____

_____

Sometimes, facing disapproval is unavoidable and can hurt. Take a moment to close your eyes and picture yourself one year from now. In this future scenario, you didn't go after your goal because you were worried about what someone would think about you. How does your future self feel? Was it worth not following what's in your heart? What advice would your future self give to you in the present about pushing through that disapproval?

_____

_____

_____

_____

_____

_____

_____

_____

_____

_____

I joyfully elevate my personal truth above a sea of oppositional opinions.

Confidence is the trust you have in yourself to overcome challenges and succeed. Think about three people who are very confident. How do they behave that makes them seem confident? When faced with a challenge, how do they behave to achieve success? What can you model from them that would help you be more confident and overcome a current challenge?

_____

_____

_____

_____

_____

_____

_____

_____

_____

_____

_____

Confidence involves trusting yourself. Think of a time you felt very confident. What role did trusting yourself play in feeling that way? What were some reasons you were able to trust yourself at that time? What's one thing you can do today to instill greater trust in yourself?

_____

_____

_____

_____

_____

_____

_____

_____

_____

_____

_____

_____

Confidence can be boosted to help you succeed. Think of one goal you're currently working on and rate your confidence level to achieve it (1 being no confidence and 10 being complete confidence). Why did you choose this number? What is preventing this number from being higher? How can you increase this number through your words, thoughts, and concrete actions?

My confidence level number is: ☐

_____

_____

_____

_____

_____

_____

_____

_____

_____

_____

_____

You become more self-confident when you achieve goals, even small ones that may seem trivial. These small successes release a feel-good neurochemical called dopamine throughout your body. This release of dopamine boosts your confidence to achieve more. In the space provided, identify two small things you can easily achieve each morning. For example, it could be "drink one liter of water and make my bed." Be consistent and enjoy the feeling of accomplishing those small successes for how they motivate you in incremental but important ways.

This morning, I can simply achieve _____

and _____

by doing _____ .

"*I was always looking outside myself for strength and confidence, but it comes from within. It is there all the time.*"

—Anna Freud

Think about the phrase "I am . . ." and focus on how powerful it can be, because whatever follows reveals a piece of your identity. In that light, the words you say after "I am . . ." are the most important words you speak. Your identity drives your behaviors, so if you say "I am a musician," you're more likely to make time to practice your instrument. When you think to yourself and say "I am . . .," what are the words that follow? How can you shift your actions to become more that person?

To achieve a goal, you'll have to expand your identity in small, practical ways that align with your greater goals. When I recorded my first album with a band I used to play with, I began by telling myself, "I am a musician." I set up the small achievable goal to write one song every three days to reinforce my new identity. What's your goal? What identity would you have to take on? What's one small action you can do every day to reinforce this identity?

_____

_____

_____

_____

_____

_____

_____

_____

_____

_____

_____

When expanding your identity, it's normal to get derailed from achieving your goal. When feeling stuck, ask yourself, "What would [your expanded identity] do in this situation?" For example, someone training for the Olympics who didn't feel like training one day could ask, "What would an Olympian do in this situation?" Thinking ahead, write three things that could derail you and how you would get back on track using this new perspective.

_____

_____

_____

_____

_____

_____

_____

_____

_____

_____

_____

_____

_____

_____

Get ready for a bit of role-playing. To begin, write out all the characteristics of the identity that will help you achieve your goal. This includes appearance, facial expression, posture, and behaviors.

_____

_____

_____

_____

_____

_____

_____

_____

_____

_____

_____

_____

_____

Next, look at an empty chair and clearly imagine your new identity sitting there. Once your visualization is clear and defined, gently sit in that chair, close your eyes, and inhabit the new identity. Allow yourself to linger in those feelings and imagine yourself as the new identity achieving your goal. How do you feel uniting your current self with this new perspective?

_____

_____

_____

_____

_____

_____

_____

_____

_____

_____

_____

Your life purpose should be the reason you get out of bed every morning. When you don't know your life purpose, you will be at the whim of other people's agendas. Living your life purpose will fulfill you and get you through tough times. Ponder these questions broadly for a moment and reflect on them for this entry: Why do you believe you're here on earth? What do you believe is your life purpose? In the bigger picture of your life, what brings you meaning?

_____

_____

_____

_____

_____

_____

_____

_____

_____

_____

_____

Passion is the activating fuel for your life purpose. Having passion means that you care and that you're willing to stick with something for the long haul and grow from your experiences. What do you really care about? What can you talk about for hours with other people? What moves you? How is your unique and individual passion connected to your life purpose?

I feel whole when my actions are in alignment with my life purpose.

Your legacy is what people will remember you by. Your legacy is what you leave behind on earth, whether it's something you've created or how you made people feel. Living your life purpose will create a legacy you will feel proud about. Imagine yourself in the future, after you've achieved all your dreams. How do you want your family, friends, and society to remember you?

_____

_____

_____

_____

_____

_____

_____

_____

_____

_____

_____

Create a personal mission statement. This will be the guiding light for your behaviors, your hope for the future, and what you stand for. Read your personal mission statement to yourself five times before you go to sleep at night so that it becomes part of your subconscious mind. Here are some suggestions to include in your mission statement:

YOUR LIFE PURPOSE

YOUR LEGACY

YOUR CALLING

YOUR IDENTITY

WHAT MAKES YOU FULFILLED

YOUR MAIN GOAL

WHOM YOU WANT TO IMPACT

YOUR PASSIONS

HOW YOU WILL ADD VALUE TO OTHER PEOPLE'S LIVES

What is your mission statement? Reflect upon how it can bring more clarity, purpose, and motivation to your life.

_____

_____

_____

_____

_____

_____

Successful organizations implement SMART goals. SMART is an acronym that stands for **S**pecific (What do you want to accomplish?), **M**easurable (How much? How many?), **A**chievable (Is this realistic?), **R**elevant (Is this worthwhile?), and **T**ime-bound (When is the deadline?).

Use the SMART formula to create your goals. An example for an author might be:

S: Write a chapter of my draft

M: 300 words per day

A: It's achievable because I can set aside two hours every day

R: Yes, because my dream is to be a published author

T: Two weeks

_____

_____

_____

_____

_____

_____

_____

A "stretch goal" asks you to go beyond your original target by thinking big! This involves getting outside your comfort zone and thinking long-term. For example, a performer might have the stretch goal of selling out concert venues even though they are currently performing in coffee shops. The key is to break down a stretch goal into multiple SMART goals. What's your stretch goal? Create two SMART goals that will help you progress toward achieving your stretch goal.

_____

_____

_____

_____

_____

_____

_____

_____

_____

_____

Morning routines are an essential part of success. What you do first thing in the morning sets the state of your mind and body throughout the day. My mentor taught me the farmer's morning routine as one valuable approach, because farmers do what's necessary first thing in the morning, like milking the cows. Embracing a routine sets up your mind and body for success. After you wake up, what can you do first thing in the morning that will have the greatest impact toward your goal?

Distractions can prevent your dreams from coming true! It's natural for humans to move toward pleasure and away from pain. When something is boring, scary, or difficult, we search for a pleasurable distraction for a jolt of dopamine, the brain's pleasure neurotransmitter. What emotion do you avoid by distracting yourself? Circle the distractions that are interfering with your current goal, and write in any others that aren't shown:

SMARTPHONE
NOTIFICATIONS

SOCIAL MEDIA

VIDEO GAMES

DAYDREAMING

CONSTANT SNACKING

SUBSTITUTING ONE TASK
FOR ANOTHER

_____   _____   _____

Making mindful changes to your environment will help motivate you to work on your goals and set you up for even more success. Look at the list of distractions you created in the previous activity, and figure out some ways to make them less accessible. For example, you could place your smartphone out of sight, remove all snacks from your house, or distance yourself from people who interrupt you while you're working. Through these kinds of environmental changes, your motivation and energy will be reserved for completing your goal.

World-class performers all have one thing in common: boundless energy. From Serena Williams to Beyoncé, they're able to keep energy levels high enough to achieve their goals. On a scale from 1 to 10 (1 feeling like a sloth and 10 feeling like a jackrabbit), how would you rate your average energy level during the week? Reflect on how your energy ebbs and flows throughout the day. At what time during the day do you have the most energy to focus on your goals? What can you do to block out that time of day where you have the most energy so that you're not interrupted or distracted?

| 1 | 2 | 3 | 4 | 5 | 6 | 7 | 8 | 9 | 10 |

_____

_____

_____

_____

_____

_____

_____

_____

Circle all of the things that are draining your energy:

EXCESSIVE SUGAR   LACK OF SLEEP   IMBALANCED DIET   EXCESSIVE CAFFEINE

EXCESSIVE ALCOHOL   TOXIC RELATIONSHIPS   EXERCISE (TOO LITTLE OR TOO MUCH)   OVERCOMMITTED SCHEDULE

EXCESSIVE SCREEN TIME   DEHYDRATION   CLUTTER AND DISORGANIZATION   EXCESSIVE MEDIA

CONSUMPTION   MULTITASKING   EXCESSIVE CRITICIZING/ COMPLAINING   _____

To increase my energy, today I will *eliminate* . . . _____

To increase my energy, today I will *add* . . . _____

If tired, I will restore my energy levels by . . . _____

Tonight, I will prepare my body and mind to be energized for tomorrow by . . .

_____

_____

_____

Creating motivational triggers will boost your energy. In this exercise, write down one motivational message to yourself that's related to your goal. Next, set up three alarms on your phone that will go off at different times of the day. When the alarm does go off, you will read your motivational message to yourself. This can be as simple as "Keep going!" or more complex and focused—for example, a person who dreams of starting their own business might set an alarm at seven a.m. and then read their message: "Achieving this goal brings me closer to freedom!"

Being courageous means to take action despite feeling fearful in the face of adversity. This struggle is an important and inevitable part of achieving your goals. What adversity have you overcome despite feeling fearful? Thinking about your current goal, complete these sentences:

A fear that comes up for me is . . .

_____

_____

_____

The positive outcome that will occur from overcoming this fear is . . .

_____

_____

_____

I can change my perspective of this fear to . . .

_____

_____

I will approach this fear by . . .

_____

_____

When you feel like giving up, it's helpful to tap in to your emotional reservoir for hidden drive and resilience. Begin by answering the following questions: What were some of your past victories? Who are some people who doubted you in the past, but you've proven them wrong? What's your proudest accomplishment? When you feel like giving up, close your eyes and remember those moments for emotional fuel. Chances are, by reflecting on that hidden drive, your mind will go from "this is impossible" to "I can do this!"

I hold all the power that I need inside me and know that I am good enough.

PART TWO

CONNECT TO WHAT MATTERS

Dreams are fueled by passion, made into reality by talent and skill, and nurtured through relationships. In order to achieve our goals, we must first connect with who we truly are and the things we care about.

We are most fulfilled when we're living a life congruent with our authentic selves. In this part you're going to cultivate and unleash your authentic self. You will use the power of motivation to identify and reflect on your talents, passions, skills, relationships, and notions of success to pave the way for fulfillment. By harnessing your strengths and bolstering your skills, you will be preparing yourself for part 3, where you will explore ways to extend your motivated self into your community and into the world.

"One isn't necessarily born with courage, but one is born with potential. Without courage, we cannot practice any other virtue with consistency. We can't be kind, true, merciful, generous, or honest."

—Maya Angelou

Childhood is one of the most formative times for your personality development. Answer the following questions: Who were your childhood best friends, and how did they shape your personality? What made you close to each other? What kind of imaginative play and creative activities would you engage in? How can you bring a similar kind of creativity and joy into your current relationships?

_____

_____

_____

_____

_____

_____

_____

_____

_____

_____

_____

_____

We all have innate strengths. What came naturally to you in early childhood? What easily grabbed your attention? Why do you think those things captivated you? What were the strengths that you first recognized within yourself? As a more mature person now, how can you leverage those innate strengths to achieve your present-day goals?

_____

_____

_____

_____

_____

_____

_____

_____

_____

_____

_____

_____

_____

_____

Psychologist Erik Erikson theorized that a majority of our identity formation occurs during adolescence. He believed that our identity is largely reinforced by social groups and peers during that time of our life. What groups or cliques did you belong to in adolescence? What was your group of peers known for? What aspects of your adolescent self do you still identify with? What advice would you give to your adolescent self? Who comprises your group of friends in the present?

_____

_____

_____

_____

_____

_____

_____

_____

_____

_____

_____

_____

In a quiet moment, recall a time from your youth when you were joyfully absorbed in play, whether that means physical activity, role-playing, engagement in music or art, building or arranging toys, or playing a game of any sort. Meditate on how you felt in that moment. Keep this feeling in your mental tool kit, and the next time you are trying to overcome a challenge related to your goal, access this feeling before brainstorming about how to proceed.

When people think of the word "talented," the image of an artist or athlete may come to mind, but that's just one way to think of it. Talent is a foundation upon which we develop skills in order to achieve mastery. Identify one of your talents that will help you achieve your goals. Then think about ways you can develop the skills associated with this talent. Can you read books on the topic? Can you take a class or development course? Does your workplace offer training? Does your local library or community center offer relevant classes or events? Are there people you know who are especially accomplished in this area that you can talk to or who can mentor you?

_____

_____

_____

_____

_____

_____

_____

_____

_____

_____

"I believe talent is like electricity. We don't understand electricity. We use it."

—Maya Angelou

Psychologist Angela Duckworth discovered in her research that incorporating your passions into your goals makes you more likely to achieve them. She found this to sometimes be more important than someone's IQ. By doing this, you'll find the process more fun, more meaningful, and more motivating. To explore what you're passionate about, start by reflecting on the things that evoke positive emotions inside of you. What are those things? How can you incorporate them into your goals?

You are passionate about something when your full attention and physical presence are immersed in the experience. Often, time goes by faster, and you feel intrinsically rewarded. What are some experiences you've had that you felt fully immersed in? What are activities you've engaged in where time went by quickly and you felt intrinsically rewarded? How can you incorporate those experiences and feelings into your current goals?

In this exercise, you will practice the loving-kindness meditation, a practice that will increase your empathy and a sense of connection to others.

As you sit in a comfortable position with your eyes closed, imagine being gathered together with your loved ones with whom you want to share love and kindness. See their faces open and honest, smiling and receptive to this loving-kindness from you.

Say this phrase to them: *"May you live with ease, may you be happy, may you be free from pain."* Finally, expand your awareness to all beings and send loving-kindness by repeating the phrase to them.

I nurture my relationships because we are all connected.

Who are your closest friends? In what ways are you most open and honest with each other? How much inspiration and emotional support to achieve your goals would you say your close friends provide for you? How are you inspiring and providing emotional support for them in return?

_____

_____

_____

_____

_____

_____

_____

_____

_____

_____

_____

_____

_____

Jim Rohn, a noted motivational speaker, once stated, "You are the average of the five people you spend the most time with." Who are the five people you spend the most time with at this point in your life? What specific, practical actions do they take to support you? Do their actions help you get closer to your goals? Which of these actions can you adopt to support your own success, as well as the success of your valuable five and others who surround you?

1. _____

2. _____

3. _____

4. _____

5. _____

_____

_____

_____

_____

_____

"Creativity is, for me, the way I share my soul with the world."

–Brené Brown

When psychologist Mihaly Csikszentmihaly interviewed 91 highly successful people, he discovered that creativity was a common characteristic they all shared. From rethinking problem-solving to expressing your ideas more robustly, creativity is necessary to bring life to whatever it is you set out to do. Answer the following questions: How have you brought creativity into your home or workspace in the past? How have you recently used creativity to solve a problem? In your current projects, how are you imprinting your authentic and creative self onto them?

_____

_____

_____

_____

_____

_____

_____

_____

_____

_____

Find three pictures of people who have used creative means to achieve what you want to achieve. It's best if the person is showing their accomplishment in the picture. Next, place those images in places where you will frequently see them, like on your computer desktop background or taped to your mirror. Frequent exposure to these images inspires your subconscious mind and imprints the fact that your goal is achievable.

Every material object on earth started in someone's imagination. Creating a tangible result will motivate you to create more, knowing that you have the power to materialize what's in your imagination. You become enlivened by this process when you share your creative thoughts with the world. Complete these sentences:

I will express my creativity more at work or within my home by . . . _____

_____

_____

_____

This week I will share my creative endeavors by . . . _____

_____

_____

_____

What I'm creating will first be shared with _____

_____ because . . .

_____

_____

_____

Embodying resilience means that you can bounce back from adversity or setbacks and continue on your path. When in your past were you able to bounce back from a setback? What kind of adversity did you experience that you overcame? What activity or responsibility do you currently feel like quitting but also know that you really want to succeed with?

_____

_____

_____

_____

_____

_____

_____

_____

_____

_____

_____

_____

At its heart, integrity simply means being honest and doing the right thing. When going about achieving your goals, why is it important for you to act with integrity? Was there a time when you didn't act with integrity to achieve a goal? If so, how did that make you feel? How does it feel to act with integrity, and what can you gain by using it as one of the guiding points on your inner motivational compass?

_____

_____

_____

_____

_____

_____

_____

_____

_____

_____

_____

_____

I become more trustworthy when I speak with honesty and act with integrity.

As frustrating as it can be in the moment, delaying short-term gratification for long-term benefits is a key component to success. Immediate gratification has its place because it relieves stress, but long-term success will be harder to achieve if you embrace that immediacy too often. When did you resist short-term gratification for long-term success? What did you do and say to yourself to stop that impulse? What's one current situation where you're giving in to short-term gratification? What would be the benefits for you to delay short-term gratification?

_____

_____

_____

_____

_____

_____

_____

_____

_____

_____

Authenticity means being real, genuine, and true about yourself. It involves knowing how you feel and sharing how you feel with others in a way that is open and honest. When do you feel like you're being most authentic? What is one example of you being authentic in your own way? How will being authentic benefit you and help keep you motivated?

_____

_____

_____

_____

_____

_____

_____

_____

_____

_____

_____

_____

At the heart of authenticity is being vulnerable. One of the best ways of expressing your vulnerability is to ask yourself, "What am I hiding about myself right now?" and then to reveal whatever you're hiding in a way that is safe for you but pushes your own boundaries and inspires growth.

In this exercise, write down one small thing you're currently hiding about yourself from someone. Next, express that truth about yourself to the person you're hiding it from. No need to start with a big vulnerability or pressure yourself about something you aren't ready to share yet. Start with something smaller that you feel ready to share about yourself.

_____

_____

_____

_____

_____

_____

_____

_____

"Vulnerability is not winning or losing; it's having the courage to show up and be seen when we have no control over the outcome. Vulnerability is not weakness; it's our greatest measure of courage."

—Brené Brown

Humility means you can acknowledge and admit to yourself and to others that you don't have all the answers. At its core, it means that you are open to listening and learning from others. Humility is like leaving your ego at the door before entering a room and putting the spotlight not begrudgingly but enthusiastically upon others. Answer the following questions: When have you acted with humility, and how has it helped you? When have you not acted with humility, and how did it not help you? How can humility help you achieve your current goals?

_____

_____

_____

_____

_____

_____

_____

_____

_____

_____

_____

_____

Practicing humility involves not making yourself the center of attention. In this exercise, you're going to make someone else the focal point of praise and celebration. Who is one person you can reach out to that deserves praise and attention? What can you do, either publicly or just on a personal level, to make this person feel praised, appreciated, acknowledged, or celebrated?

Curiosity is an intrinsic motivator that drives you to explore, seek answers, and resolve uncertainty.

Thinking about your goal, what are three things that stir up the most curiosity for you?

1. _____

2. _____

3. _____

What can you do to explore and seek answers to what you're curious about in relation to your goal?

1. _____

2. _____

3. _____

What can you do with those answers to the questions you're curious about to further the achievement of your goal?

_____

_____

_____

I actively follow my curiosity about people and the world to lead my mind into wondrous places I would never have imagined.

Much like how seeds can grow into trees, humans follow a trajectory of growth and change. Tapping in to your abilities to learn and adapt, because you also are ever-growing and changing, what is a skill you want to develop? How will this skill help you achieve your goal?

_____

_____

_____

_____

_____

_____

_____

_____

_____

_____

_____

_____

_____

Active listening is a valuable technique used in therapy and everyday life. It involves fully concentrating and making clarifying statements to ensure that you fully understand what the other person is saying. When was the last time you actively listened to someone without interruptions or impatiently awaiting your turn to speak? How did that person respond to your total, intentional presence with them? Consider someone you know who wants to be heard. How can you give them your full attention?

_____

_____

_____

_____

_____

_____

_____

_____

_____

_____

When you're actively listening to someone, the speaker engages with you more, and in return, you engage more with them. For this exercise, play a video clip, from the news or any video you like, where two people are having a conversation. Focus on one of the people and the statements they make in the clip. Practice the following active listening phrases by pausing the video and responding to them:

What I'm hearing you say is . . . [summarize the speaker's statement] _____

_____

_____

_____

Correct me if I'm wrong, but what you're saying is . . . [summarize the speaker's

statement] _____

_____

_____

_____

Sharing what you create with the world can be nerve-racking, but it's an essential part of adding value to the lives of others. In this exercise, share your creative idea or project with two people whom you feel might be most receptive to your work. If it's not completed yet, that's okay, because you're looking for honest feedback from people you trust and whose opinions you respect.

Reach out to them through a phone call or email or in person, and listen to their responses with an open, intentional mind. Decide whether the feedback adds value to your ideas; then, if your idea should be modified, apply the knowledge you gained from the process.

Growing up, we often have heroes and people we look up to, whether they're family members or friends, coaches, teachers, or even our favorite actors on the movie screen. They can all embody different qualities we admire. As your younger self, whom did you look up to? Why did you admire them? Whom do you currently look up to? What habits or behaviors do these people display that you think would help you get closer to achieving your current goal?

_____

_____

_____

_____

_____

_____

_____

_____

_____

_____

Great ideas occur when you're out in the world interacting with others. Like an anthropologist, you have to go out in the field and observe people, learning from their strengths, differences, and interactions. Thinking about a time when you were inspired by someone engaging in their craft, what were they doing and why did it inspire you? Where do you go now to observe people for inspiration? What kinds of questions can you ask those people, whether in real life or in online communities, to help you move forward?

_____

_____

_____

_____

_____

_____

_____

_____

_____

_____

_____

"*Some people arrive and make such a beautiful impact on your life, you can barely remember what life was like without them.*"

—Anna Taylor

In order to have fulfilling relationships that meet your needs, you have to make a conscious effort to create them. What defines a good relationship for you? What kinds of relationships do you want now, in this chapter of your life? What would you have to do to create new relationships that fulfill your current needs? How can you deepen those new relationships in a way that is meaningful?

_____

_____

_____

_____

_____

_____

_____

_____

_____

_____

_____

Thinking about your current closest relationships, what qualities do these people bring to your relationships? Which of these qualities are you most grateful for and why? What qualities do you bring to these relationships that you believe they are grateful for?

_____

_____

_____

_____

_____

_____

_____

_____

_____

_____

_____

_____

_____

Understanding how others perceive you is one way to gauge how you're creating an impact on their lives. This helps direct and center your motivation, because it gives you feedback on whether your actions should change or stay the course to achieve the impact you want in other people's lives.

What are three things people notice about your personality when they first meet you?

1. _____

2. _____

3. _____

What are three things you wished people could know about you when they first meet you?

1. _____

2. _____

3. _____

How can you put to the forefront the qualities you wished people knew about you?

_____

_____

_____

To manifest your large goals, you might find it helpful to have allies who share your vision. Accountability, supportive feedback, and group brainstorming can help move your goal forward.

In this exercise, think of three people who share your interests. Contact them and share your vision. If they're enthusiastic about it, ask them to join you, in some capacity, in your pursuit of this goal. If not, consider their feedback and how you might incorporate it into your goal in a productive, positive way.

Engagement with those who have achieved mastery in the skills and abilities you value most is highly motivating. Meaningful interactions can occur in a variety of settings, from a meeting or informational interview to asking questions at public events, online seminars, book signings, or lectures. You will get more out of your interaction if you have thought through your questions before asking them. Brainstorm a series of thoughtful questions that you could ask someone who has achieved something similar to what you want to achieve. Avoid questions that can be answered with a simple yes or no, or common questions that can be answered by reading published interviews or biographical material.

_____

_____

_____

_____

_____

_____

_____

_____

_____

In the pursuit of adding value to other people's lives, it's possible to overextend yourself and neglect your own needs or motivational milestones in the process. Write about a time when you overextended yourself. What lessons about meeting your needs can you take away from that experience? How will you meet your needs first while also adding value to others' lives and experiences at the same time?

_____

_____

_____

_____

_____

_____

_____

_____

_____

_____

_____

_____

_____

_____

When you are focused on the intricacies of achieving complex or long-term goals, self-care can easily fall by the wayside. But without adequate self-care, you might feel burned out, exhausted, and lose your motivation. Take a few minutes for a quick self-care check-in. Do you get the ideal amount of sleep your body needs? If not, how can you adjust your routine to get the sleep you need? Are you eating healthy foods and drinking enough water? What physical issues do you need to attend to rather than putting them off for a later date? What can you do to get enough time with people who care about you? What's one thing you can do to better manage your emotions?

_____

_____

_____

_____

_____

_____

_____

_____

_____

Having the right ratio between meeting your needs and the needs of those around you is important. After all, you can't spend all your emotional resources on others and leave yourself with nothing to fuel your own goals. Write down two boundaries you are willing to commit to today so that you are meeting your needs first and not overextending yourself.

Today, I will set boundaries with _____ and

_____

I will set these boundaries by saying _____

_____

_____

and doing _____

_____

_____

I will meet my needs first by doing _____

_____

_____

_____

Large goals, and our dreams of achieving them, can be thrilling, but they can also be intimidating. In order to maintain your motivation while working toward complex goals, it's critical to remember that they comprise a series of smaller steps. Think about your large goal, then break it down into smaller steps. These steps should be small enough that you can realistically do at least one every day in order to maintain and build your motivation toward the accomplishment of your overall goal.

_____

_____

_____

_____

_____

_____

_____

_____

_____

_____

_____

_____

_____

Right now, you may think you'll feel accomplished only after you've met your big goals, but the truth is that regular small wins are integral to your sense of success. It's important to intentionally notice the small wins every day. What were some small wins you had last week? What were some small wins you had yesterday? What were some small wins you had today?

When you mentor someone, you become a source of inspiration for your mentee and are partially responsible for their learning. The relationship can be highly motivating, because you don't want to let your mentee down. Who were your mentors in the past? How did they motivate you and others by drawing on their life experiences? Why would it be beneficial for you to mentor someone?

_____

_____

_____

_____

_____

_____

_____

_____

_____

_____

_____

I make a difference in the world by happily sharing my skills and talents with others.

PART THREE

GREET THE WORLD AS THE RADIANT YOU

Throughout your journaling, you've been digging deep and taking action on becoming the most motivated version of yourself through openness, reflection, and honesty.

In this final part, you are going to show up to the world by becoming your most radiant self! After all, people are so often remembered by how they left others feeling and how they contributed to their communities in their own special ways.

Having a meaningful impact on people's lives is what drove Dr. Martin Luther King Jr. to pursue and take powerful action about civil rights and equality, and it's what led Malala Yousafzai to become an outspoken human rights advocate. People like Dr. King and Malala are self-actualized, meaning that they are living up to their unique human potential. The final part of this journal is about you contributing to your community and the world in a way that brings out your special and most motivated self, because nobody has the same combination of skills, talents, and gifts that you do. Within this section, you will explore your relationship to your communities as well as take practical action on a positive vision for the community you wish to be a part of and leave behind for future generations.

"The greatness of a community is most accurately measured by the compassionate actions of its members."

—Coretta Scott King

Think about a cause that is very important to you, whether it's something humanitarian, social, or political, or something else. What causes are you willing to stand up for? Why are these causes important to you? Why do these causes motivate you? Where in your community do you see opportunities to use your strengths for these causes?

_____

_____

_____

_____

_____

_____

_____

_____

_____

_____

_____

_____

If you had all the resources in the world, what person or group of people would you first help? How would you help them? Looking at your life today, what's one small and realistic thing you can do to extend a helping hand to that person or group of people?

_____

_____

_____

_____

_____

_____

_____

_____

_____

_____

_____

_____

An act of kindness is like the glue of society, providing us perspective and tangible proof that good people exist in the world. What was one act of kindness you did in the past for another person? How did the person react and feel after your act of kindness? What is one act of kindness you can do today? Why do you think this act of kindness is important to others? How will it affect their lives for the better?

_____

_____

_____

_____

_____

_____

_____

_____

_____

_____

_____

_____

_____

"Pay It Forward" is a social movement driven by acts of kindness. It works when a person does acts of kindness to three people and asks them to each pay the favor forward. It can be as simple as letting someone go ahead of you in a line or paying for a stranger's coffee. The goal is to create an exponential effect of good deeds. Think of three opportunities where you can do an act of kindness. If you feel comfortable, use those opportunities to let the person know that they can pay it forward by doing acts of kindness for three other people.

Life is all about defining moments. For me, a defining moment in my life was when a good friend was diagnosed with obsessive-compulsive disorder. It was an epiphany that changed my life because it led me down a path of learning about mental health and becoming a psychologist. What was a defining moment that changed your life path in a positive direction? How can you draw on your defining moments to change the lives of people in your community in a positive direction?

_____

_____

_____

_____

_____

_____

_____

_____

_____

_____

_____

"There is no power for change greater than that of a community discovering what it cares about."

—Margaret J. Wheatley

Remember the traditions from your upbringing? You may have liked or disliked some of those traditions, but you can probably respect their intention: to bring people together for a greater purpose. What traditions did your family or circle have that you were motivated to partake in? Why would having traditions in your community motivate greater cohesion and purpose? How can you bring a valued tradition, new or old, into a community you belong to?

_____

_____

_____

_____

_____

_____

_____

_____

_____

_____

_____

A community is a group of people who share similar customs, identities, and values. What does community mean to you? What communities have you belonged to in the past or currently? Is there a community you would like to join or help create, and if so, what is it and why is it important to you?

It's important that you narrow down your focus on the populations and communities that you can best serve, since it concentrates your message and actions to their most potent forms. In this exercise, you will get a clearer understanding of who you'll focus on for the greatest impact. Step into their shoes and answer these questions about the specific group you want to engage:

What are their values? What books or movies or social media do they enjoy? What are their age ranges and genders? Do they have large families and friend circles or smaller ones? Where do they work, or play, or live? Write or draw responses to these questions, tapping in to your knowledge about these communities as well as your own creativity, fun, and sense of imaginative play.

I freely add value to people's lives knowing that value will return to me when I least expect it.

How can you make your fellow community members feel most valued? How can you show gratitude to them? How can you make appreciation a common part of the cultures you're involved with on a daily basis?

_____

_____

_____

_____

_____

_____

_____

_____

_____

_____

_____

_____

Charity donations involve sharing some of your resources, whether financial, material, time-based, or otherwise, with others. This could be anything from giving away unworn or gently used clothes to donating canned food from your pantry. Have you ever donated to a charity? If so, why did you choose to donate to them? How can you incorporate donations and charity as a part of your goals? Why would incorporating charity into your regular practice be a beneficial idea?

> *"Those who are happiest are those who do the most for others."*
>
> *—Booker T. Washington*

Between the ages of 17 and 23, I was a volunteer at a psychiatric hospital, an undertaking that helped me be more involved in the mental health community and changed me by answering the question of whether I should become a psychologist. Have you volunteered for an organization? If so, why did you choose to volunteer for them? If you haven't volunteered in the past, is there an organization you'd be interested in volunteering with? In what ways would volunteering with that organization help you achieve your own goals?

_____

_____

_____

_____

_____

_____

_____

_____

_____

_____

_____

Political acceptance speeches involve addressing the issues voters care about most and outlining how politicians will solve those problems. In this exercise, imagine you are elected to be the mayor of your town or city and you have to give an acceptance speech. Go into your community and observe the issues the citizens in your city are most concerned about. What issues did you see that need to be addressed, and how would you solve them?

To take a stand for something means that you unwaveringly express your opinion on it despite other people's opposition. What have you intentionally taken a stand for in the past? Why was that important to you? What would you take a stand for now? Why is this important to you? How is this related to the larger vision you see for change both within your life and for those around you?

_____

_____

_____

_____

_____

_____

_____

_____

_____

_____

_____

_____

_____

Trust is the belief that people can depend on you. If you're going to enter their lives and take an active role in the community, people need to first trust you. What does trust mean to you personally? Who are the people or organizations that you trust the most? What are their qualities and actions that allow you to trust them? What can you do to gain the trust of others and the community you want to serve?

_____

_____

_____

_____

_____

_____

_____

_____

_____

_____

_____

_____

_____

_____

Part of participating in your community is presenting yourself as a role model. Complete the following prompts about being a role model:

If I want to be a better role model in my community, I will start by doing . . .

_____

_____

_____

The people in my community who most need me to be a good role model are . . .

_____

_____

_____

I can be a reliable role model for those people by doing . . .

_____

_____

In one year from now, I would like to be described as a role model in my community by things like . . .

_____

_____

"Of all the judgments we pass in life, none is more important as the one we pass on ourselves."

—Nathaniel Branden

This exercise is called the mapping technique and is based in Internal Family Systems Therapy. It allows you to tap in to different parts of your subconscious that make up who you are and will help you gain more insight into the part of you that is a leader.

To begin, read the steps and then start the exercise:

1. Close your eyes and imagine yourself being a leader in your ideal community. What does it look like for you?

2. With your eyes still closed, see yourself as that leader interacting with your community, and sit with the emotion that comes up for you.

3. Allow that emotion to guide your mind to the first image of a symbol that represents the emotion.

4. Open your eyes and draw that symbol in the space provided.

5. Write about the meaning of that symbol and how it relates to you being a leader.

Seeking to understand people's dreams and concerns will help you become a better leader. This is because leadership, as the leadership expert John Maxwell believes, is about serving others first. Think about the people who belong to the community that you want to uplift. What do you believe their dreams are? What do you believe keeps them up at night? How can you use your leadership skills and abilities to get them closer to achieving their dreams?

_____

_____

_____

_____

_____

_____

_____

_____

_____

Being a leader involves applying interpersonal skills like active listening (page 88) and communicating clearly in larger group settings. Think about a leader who excels at facilitating community dialogue. How do they validate input and synthesize comments and feedback in order to make individuals feel heard? How do they respectfully clarify their understanding of the problem before offering solutions? Using this person's skills as a model along with your earlier insights into active listening and clear communication, brainstorm a few speaking and listening strategies that will help you foster productive community dialogue.

Think about the communities you are most involved with. What are their unique strengths? What makes your community special and different from others that have similar qualities? What could you do in your own way to make them even more cohesive and stronger?

_____

_____

_____

_____

_____

_____

_____

_____

_____

_____

_____

_____

I proudly live my life as an example of how I want to see people interact with one another in my community.

All civilizations have changed over time from advancements in technology, changes in laws and social norms, and even catastrophes such as pandemics. It's inevitable that your most cherished community will also change. What's your vision of positive change for your community's future? What role do you want to take on in your community's changes? What is one small thing you can do to start making positive changes in your community? In the future, what do you want your community to be known for?

_____

_____

_____

_____

_____

_____

_____

_____

_____

_____

The beauty of working within a diverse group is that there is a wide range of perspectives. Because of this, conflicts may arise on how to steer the course toward a goal. One approach to resolving this conflict would be to find compromises, which are mutual agreements. Think of current possible conflicts toward achieving a goal within your group. What are the points of agreement and common ground? What are some opposing perspectives? What solutions would benefit everyone?

When it comes to compromise, all parties involved must sacrifice something to reach an agreement. Think of the United Nations having to make a decision with so many different countries weighing in; if there's enough of a win-win for everyone, relationships are maintained. Think of a negotiation that needs to be reached in your community. What can you sacrifice to create a win-win compromise? What can you propose that other parties should sacrifice for a win-win compromise?

A walking meditation begins with the commitment of being mindfully present with your surroundings as you walk from one place to another. The key is to have no distractions. Choose a place in your community where you feel safe to walk alone for five minutes. Bring your attention to your surroundings. Reflect on what you appreciate about your community, what you may have taken for granted, and what you see while walking that you can help improve.

"As you discover what strength you can draw from your community in this world from which it stands apart, look outward as well as inward. Build bridges instead of walls."

—Associate Justice Sonia Sotomayor

For communities to thrive and progress, it's important that they are flexible and ever-evolving. What social norms in your community have changed over time? Why were those changes beneficial for the community? What would you change about those social norms so that they benefit the progress of your community? What might be the opposition to change, and how could you respectfully counter that, coming from a place of love and compassion?

Communities grow and improve when the people within them are challenged in a respectful manner, instead of an oppositional one, because it calls people to work together in a unifying, cohesive manner. How have you been challenged in life about issues that helped you grow? How were you approached by others so that you accepted the challenge? How can you challenge your community members, in a respectful way that's rooted in love and kindness, to improve and to grow?

_____

_____

_____

_____

_____

_____

_____

_____

_____

_____

_____

In this exercise, you are going to work with your community to help raise public awareness on an important issue. Answer these questions, then take action!

1. An issue that is a concern to my community is ...

2. The people in my community who can help raise public awareness are ...

Choose a medium to raise public awareness through, then take action on it. Examples might include getting active on social media, planning fundraisers, fostering community outreach through education, or attending or planning public demonstrations.

A community becomes more cohesive, and interconnected with other communities, through contribution. When communities are more motivated, their contribution increases. Complete these prompts about your role in contributing to your community:

The greatest contributions of the community that I'm most involved with are . . . _____

_____

_____

I would like to see my community contributing more by doing . . . __

_____

_____

I can motivate my community to connect more with other communities by doing . . . _____

_____

_____

Your community is composed of different generations and diverse groups of people of all ages and backgrounds. How can you get the younger members involved in the positive vision you have for the future? How can you get the older members involved, too? How can you encourage your community to be more accepting of and welcoming to the diversity of new and current voices within it?

When you collaborate with diverse communities, you create a unique fusion of ideas and outcomes. From the mix of hip-hop with rock 'n' roll to actors collaborating with food brands, uncommon collaborations create something special. How have you collaborated with people who work across different mediums from you? How can diverse collaborations improve the outcome of your goals?

_____

_____

_____

_____

_____

_____

_____

_____

_____

_____

I actively seek opportunities to build bridges with diverse communities for our greater good as a whole.

Struggle is an important and unavoidable part of any journey. When people are motivated to overcome struggles, that's when deeper bonds are formed among the community at large. What struggles has your community been motivated to overcome? How were bonds deepened? What's a current struggle your community is facing? What's a solution, or one step forward, you might have for that struggle?

_____

_____

_____

_____

_____

_____

_____

_____

_____

_____

The challenges your community is facing now are part of the process along the journey to something better for all. What is one challenge your community is currently facing? What is this challenge inviting you to take on for a better future? How have you faced similar challenges in the past? How will you support others as they rise to face this current challenge?

_____

_____

_____

_____

_____

_____

_____

_____

_____

_____

A social movement is a locally or globally organized campaign with a common goal. Consider the social movements that have taken place throughout history. What social movement inspired you in the past? What was it about that social movement that was important to you? What social movement currently inspires you? How can you engage with and contribute to that social movement in a small way that is authentic to you?

Writing a powerful letter or an online petition to an elected official can help create change for your community. However, your petition might not get noticed unless hundreds of people are involved. Answer these questions and then take action! If you need to, look back at the issues you'd confront if elected to your own public office (page 124) to help inspire these responses.

1. An issue that concerns my community is . . .

_____

_____

_____

2. The elected official who can help create change is . . .

_____

_____

_____

Next, write a short letter, make copies, and organize as many people as possible in your community to send it off. If you start an online petition, create a social media campaign and encourage your community to share it with others. Make sure it includes information about the problem, your request, and the main organizer's contact information.

Having perseverance means committing to your long-term goal despite setbacks. What's an example of perseverance you displayed in the past? What did you tell yourself through the difficult times to get right back up? How can you use your own experience to help the groups you're involved with recover from a setback?

Determination and hope lie at the foundation of perseverance. In all work that strives to achieve a greater good, uncertainty and disappointment are inevitable. During these times, it is important that we remind ourselves, as individuals as well as communities, what is at the core of our ambition. To strengthen your perseverance, write your responses to these prompts. Be sure to refer to these answers when you need extra motivation in a challenging time:

The reasons I want to achieve this goal are . . .

_____

_____

This goal is connected to my purpose on earth because . . .

_____

_____

I can reconnect to hope by . . .

_____

_____

I can overcome the hurdles in my path by . . .

_____

_____

I will care for myself and my community by . . .

_____

_____

By achieving this goal, I will . . .

_____

_____

The universal truth of interconnectivity is that we are all linked to everything, much like a giant spiderweb. None of us could realize our goals without interacting with other people. Today, consider reaching out to someone in your community and acknowledging them. Whether through a five-minute phone call, a handwritten note, or a thoughtfully crafted text message, make the time to acknowledge how they have touched your life. The absolute greatest gift you can give someone is seeing them for the gift they are to you.

I humbly accept, uplift, and nurture all people in my community because we are on this journey together.

RESOURCES

Online Resources and Mobile Apps

PsychologyToday.com
DayZeroProject.com
TikTok: @dr_chris10
Calm App
Strides: Goal and Habit Tracker App
ThinkUp: Positive Affirmations App

Books

Man's Search for Meaning by Viktor E. Frankl
Awaken the Giant Within: How to Take Immediate Control of Your Mental, Emotional, Physical and Financial Destiny! by Tony Robbins
High Performance Habits: How Extraordinary People Become That Way by Brendon Burchard
Can't Hurt Me: Master Your Mind and Defy the Odds by David Goggins

Podcasts

The Marie Forleo Podcast
School of Greatness Podcast with Lewis Howes
Shrink Rap Radio with David Van Nuys

REFERENCES

Angelou, Maya and Elliot, Jeffrey M., ed. *Conversations with Maya Angelou,* University Press of Mississippi, 1989.

Bachman, Justin. "King's Widow Urges Acts of Compassion." *Los Angeles Times.* January 17, 2000. https://LATimes.com/archives/la-xpm-2000-jan-17-mn-54832-story.html#:~:tex t=%E2%80%9CThe%20greatness%20of%20a%20community,a%20soul%20generated%20 by%20love.%E2%80%9D.

Branden, Nathaniel. *The Six Pillars of Self-Esteem: The Definitive Work on Self-Esteem by the Leading Pioneer in the Field.* Bantam Books, 1995.

Brown, Brené. *Rising Strong: How the Ability to Reset Transforms the Way We Live, Love, Parent, and Lead.* New York: Random House, 2015.

Brown, Brené / from "Brené Brown on 'Big Strong Magic,'" *Magic Lessons with Elizabeth Gilbert* podcast, Season 1, Episode 12. https://podcasts.apple.com/ us/podcast/magic-lessons-se-1-ep-12-brene-brown-on-big-strong-magic/ id1138081319?i=1000373139417

Caravan, Giti. *12 Key Steps to Build High Confidence: The Master Key to Your Power.* Bloomington, IN: Balboa Press, 2019.

Crockett, Chelsea. *Your Own Beautiful: Advice and Inspiration from Chelsea Crockett.* Grand Rapids, MI: Zondervan, 2017.

Deutsch, Lindsay. "13 of Maya Angelou's Best Quotes." *USA Today.* May 28, 2014. https://USA Today.com/story/news/nation-now/2014/05/28/maya-angelou-quotes/9663257.

Douglas, Arthur A. *2412 Mark Twain Quotes.* UB Tech, 2016.

Erikson, Erik H. *Identity and the Life Cycle.* New York: W. W. Norton & Co., 1994.

McGonigal, Kelly. *The Willpower Instinct: How Self-Control Works, Why it Matters, and What You Can Do to Get More of It*. New York: Penguin Group, 2013.

Obama, Michelle. *Becoming*. New York: Crown Publishing Group, 2018.

Sotomayor, Sonia. *My Beloved World*. New York: Vintage Books, 2014.

Stanford News. "'You've Got to Find What You Love,' Job Says." June 12, 2015. https://News.Stanford.edu/2005/06/14/jobs-061505.

Washington, Booker T. *Up from Slavery*. Millennium Publications, 2015.

Wheatley, Margaret J. *Turning to One Another: Simple Conversations to Restore Hope to the Future*. San Francisco: Berrett-Koehler Publishers, Inc., 2009.

The White House, Office of the First Lady. "Remarks by the First Lady at Tuskegee University Commencement Address." Last modified May 9, 2015. https://ObamaWhiteHouse.archives.gov/the-press-office/2015/05/09/remarks-first-lady-tuskegee-university-commencement-address.

Widener, Chris. *Jim Rohn's 8 Best Success Lessons*. Seattle: Made for Success, Incorporated, 2014.

ACKNOWLEDGMENTS

I have to start by thanking my parents, Corneliu and Maria Rizea, as well as my brother, Bogdan Rizea. They've always believed in me on my journey to becoming a psychologist. I love you all.

There's not enough gratitude that can go toward my loving wife, Sasha. From giving me advice on topics to supporting me throughout this writing process, she was very important to getting this book done. Thank you so much, dear.

I'd also like to thank Rafael Moiseev, Roman Dietrich, and Jonathan Wanger for their constant support throughout the years. You guys are the best!

A big thanks goes to my editor, Jesse Aylen. His expertise kept me on track, and he challenged me to think differently. Much appreciated!

Finally, I thank Callisto Media and everyone there who was involved in making this book come alive! I'm grateful for you giving me the opportunity to write this journal so that we can touch the lives of all the people who make use of it.

ABOUT THE AUTHOR

Dr. Christian Rizea, PsyD, is a licensed clinical psychologist and motivational speaker living in California. He is founder of the Dr. Chris, Life Academy, an online personal development community where its members learn to be more self-empowered, live their highest potential, and have radiant relationships. For more than a decade, his unique approaches to helping people overcome challenges and experience genuine presence has made him a sought-after keynote speaker and seminar leader. Find him online at www.DrChrisLifeAcademy.com and on Instagram at @DrChris10.